BLOCKCHAIN

A Clear and Simple Guide to the Technology That Makes Cryptocurrency Work

ALFORD BENSON

© Copyright 2018 by Author Name - All rights reserved.

The following Paperback is reproduced below with the goal of providing information that is as accurate and reliable as possible. Regardless, purchasing this eBook can be seen as consent to the fact that both the publisher and the author of this book are in no way experts on the topics discussed within and that any recommendations or suggestions that are made herein are for entertainment purposes only. Professionals should be consulted as needed prior to undertaking any of the action endorsed herein.

This declaration is deemed fair and valid by both the American Bar Association and the Committee of Publishers Association and is legally binding throughout the United States.

Furthermore, the transmission, duplication or reproduction of any of the following work including specific information will be considered an illegal act irrespective of if it is done electronically or in print. This extends to creating a secondary or tertiary copy of the work or a recorded copy and is only allowed with express written consent from the Publisher. All additional right reserved.

The information in the following pages is broadly considered to be a truthful and accurate account of facts and as such any inattention, use or misuse of the information in question by the reader will render any resulting actions solely under their purview. There are no scenarios in which the publisher or the original author of this work can be in any fashion deemed liable for any hardship or damages that may befall them after undertaking information described herein.

Additionally, the information in the following pages is intended only for informational purposes and should thus be thought of as universal. As befitting its nature, it is presented without assurance regarding its prolonged validity or interim quality. Trademarks that are mentioned are done without written consent and can in no way be considered an endorsement from the trademark holder.

Acknowledgment

I would like to give heartful thanks to my dear friend and colleague Robert Buxton who provided carefully considered feedback and valuable comments. I also owe a very important debt to Arnold Trent whose opinions and information have helped me very much throughout the production of this content.

ALFORD BENSON

This book is dedicated to my lovely wife Anne and our two daughters Mary and Julie.

Table of Contents

Acknowledgment 5
Table of Contents 7
Introduction 9
Chapter 1 What is Blockchain? 13
Chapter 2 History of Blockchain 19
Chapter 3 Blockchain Technology 25
Chapter 4 The Purpose of Blockchain 31
Chapter 5 How blockchain is currently used . 35
Chapter 6 Current Limitations and Issues 43
Chapter 7 Perspectives on Blockchain 53
Chapter 8 Smart contracts 61
Chapter 9 Decentralized Apps 73
Chapter 10 Future of Blockchain 79
Chapter 11 Blockchain Terminology 93
Conclusion 107

ALFORD BENSON

INTRODUCTION

The past decade has boasted many fascinating upgrades in the world of technology. One of the biggest and most talked about developments was Bitcoin. This was the first ever cryptocurrency that became mainstream and was used in a functional and secured manner. What many people did not realize at the time was that upon launching Bitcoin, there was also the development of an entirely new technology altogether: blockchain.

Blockchain was the protocol that made Bitcoin the first ever successful cryptocurrency. Based on this knowledge, many developers and researchers have invested themselves in understanding how this protocol can be exploited to work in a variety of environments.

Over the past decade, blockchain has been revolutionized far beyond what anyone else expected. While there are still many advancements that must be made before this protocol is completely integrated in the way that developers hope it will be, it's clear that this protocol is not going anywhere anytime soon.

If you have ever wondered what made Bitcoin possible, and why this blockchain technology is so revolutionary and exciting to people all around the world, you have found the perfect place to learn more. "Blockchain: A Clear and Simple Guide to the Technology That Makes Cryptocurrencies Work," is all about how this technology has advanced, what makes it so revolutionary, and why it's the only technology that made cryptocurrencies possible. This guide goes in-depth but will certainly keep things clear and easy to understand. So, if you are not too familiar with technology or technical terms, you will still be able to understand the concepts being introduced and the fascination with this incredible technology. If you are ready to begin exploring this protocol, the concept behind it, and the many phenomenal aspects of it, then read on. And please, enjoy!

ALFORD BENSON

CHAPTER 1
WHAT IS BLOCKCHAIN?

With the rapid increase in popularity in cryptocurrencies, especially Bitcoin, talk about the blockchain has also increased. For many people, understanding cryptocurrencies can be quite simple, but blockchain may be a little more complex to understand.

Although blockchain is commonly associated with cryptocurrency, its realm of abilities does not end there. Since its launch, blockchain has grown to be used for everything from copyright protection to electronic health records. Understanding the vast realm of possibilities associated with blockchain helps you understand that it is not so tightly entwined with the cryptocurrencies that it cannot be separated and used for its own variety of technologies.

Essentially, blockchain is a public ledger built from a variety of transactions. When it came to Bitcoin, it was designed to help validate and store transactions of the currency. This allowed it to be a secured cryptocurrency because once the transaction was approved into the blockchain, it could not be erased or reversed.

Since realizing the power of this technology, computer scientists have managed to separate it from cryptocurrencies and create many additional uses for it. Blockchain is now used to store a variety of different transactions on a public ledger that confirms that the transaction was, in fact, made and that both parties consented to the transaction. This means that once the transaction is finalized, it cannot be denied nor erased. These days, these transactions are not required to include monetary values. Instead, as previously mentioned, they may include things like the passing of a copyright protection, or consent for something else to take place between two people. Because the transactions are confirmed by both parties and irreversible, it is believed that they can be used as evidence that cannot be destroyed. This evidence can be used to protect people and ensure that legal rights and documents are upheld, such as with copyright laws.

Because of the nature of blockchain and how it permanently stores transactions which cannot be erased, and that are visible to the public, many people believe that this public ledger can be used to erase the middleman. In other words, they believe that this could be used in the financial sector to erase banks, and even in some legal cases to erase the need for lawyers. With this information permanently and publicly documented, the idea is that you would not require a third party to facilitate the official "business" to be initiated between two individuals. Instead, if the transaction is legitimate, it will be stored in the blockchain and therefore serve as permanent, public evidence that both parties agreed to either the financial transaction or the legal circumstances. Still, it should never be used in place of a lawyer or legal team. Especially not now, in a time where it is still being explored and understood.

Many people describe the blockchain as "the internet of value." Basically, the internet itself made it possible for individuals to transfer data back and forth and share it freely amongst each other. The idea is that blockchain will enable individuals to do the same with money and eventually, other forms of transactions as well. It gives the public the power to be able to do whatever they want, make any transactions they want, and freely transfer money back and forth between each other without having to use banks, or other financial institutions to facilitate the transactions.

Some people also liken blockchain to that of Google Docs. Prior to the development and launch of Google Docs, individuals had to create a Microsoft Word document and send it back and forth to allow each party to edit anything in the document. Then, they would save the changes and send it back to you. In Google Docs, however, multiple people can view and edit documents at the same time without having to do the sending-back-and-forth action. It makes it quicker, easier, and more effective for everyone involved.

With blockchain, it is quite the same. You do not have to do one transaction at a time. Instead, many people can validate transactions and the system will automatically and instantly update any changes made for everyone to see on the public ledger. This means that when you are banking with others, the transfers are verified on both ends at the same time and immediately made available for all to see.

While this is primarily used in the financial sector right now with cryptocurrencies, it is clear that this technology could easily evolve to be used in many other areas in business as well. For example, through legal business, architectural planning, and more. Essentially, anywhere that a group of people would need or want to collaborate on a document, blockchain could be used to instantaneously update changes made and inform all involved parties. This would make these practices more effective, easier to complete, and much less time-consuming.

As you can see, blockchain is a powerful technology that can be used in many ways to help facilitate transactions of information between people instantaneously. There are many metaphors that can be used to describe what blockchain is and what it does, but at the very core, it is simply a public ledger that stores transactions in a chain-like structure of data for all to see. Over time, as developers learn to understand it more and seek ways to securely and effectively integrate it into various other systems, blockchain will likely become a part of many different industries and sectors in the business world.

CHAPTER 2
HISTORY OF BLOCKCHAIN

Like all things, blockchain has an interesting history as to how it came to be. Initially, no one really recognized that this powerful technology was so revolutionary. In fact, it was simply a part of a separate technology that was released: Bitcoin. Over time, however, developers learned they could isolate this technology from Bitcoin and use it for many other purposes. Let us take a look at what the history of blockchain is and how this technology came to be in the first place.

Linked to Bitcoin

Initially, blockchain was considered to be nothing more than the original source file for Bitcoin. It was a technology developed to enable the currency to be freely and securely transferred in a peer-to-peer environment. The blockchain was used to create a security system that would prevent people from double-spending their funds or conducting otherwise fraudulent transactions between one another. After all, with a traditional banking institution, consumers are protected by a variety of protection practices enforced by the banks themselves. In a peer-to-peer currency where middlemen would not be necessary, new action would need to be taken to uphold the same, if not better, level of security.

That is how blockchain was introduced. This public ledger was designed to store transactions of Bitcoin between peers in a permanent and irreversible way. Once something is added to the blockchain, it cannot be removed or reversed. It is indestructible. This is because every subsequent block relies on the information in that particular block to be developed and added. If something was changed somewhere back in the blockchain, it would corrupt all of the subsequent blocks. That or, those blocks would need to be altered as well. This would take an incredible amount of time and power; therefore, it is considered impossible and cannot be done.

Through this system, Bitcoin was completely secured. So, essentially, blockchain was the very technology that made Bitcoin the first ever successful form of cryptocurrency. Prior to Bitcoin and blockchain, all previous attempts at cryptocurrencies were extremely unsafe and imposed a high risk of fraud that made the coins illegitimate and unusable. Without blockchain, Bitcoin would not exist either. While Bitcoin itself was a revolutionary development that became incredibly mainstream in less than a decade, it was truly blockchain that made it all possible. As people begin to recognize this, they are becoming more and more interested in the many uses of blockchain and how it may be able to revolutionize technology as a whole.

Separated from Bitcoin

Many people were curious about how the blockchain would work if it were separated from Bitcoin. After all, it was designed as a software technology that was used to support Bitcoin itself. So, would it even be realistic to separate the two? Could it happen?

Some people speculated that it would not be possible, but many more realized the potential behind this revolutionary discovery. That is, blockchain is simply a technology used to publicly store transactions. If it could be designed to support Bitcoin, then you should be able to separate it, clone the blockchain technology, and apply it to other technological designs too. Many individuals invested large amounts of cash into blockchain development to separate the technology and recreate it in a way that it would be able to be reapplied to other technologies in the future.

The biggest issue that these individuals faced, however, was that the blockchain needed something to actually transact. Blocks or tokens of some form that would resemble the transaction itself. It would need to be some form of digital transaction that had something "tangible" to be transacted across the blockchain. Otherwise, the chain would not be able to verify anything. There would be nothing to transact! For this reason, developers had to find a new way to create a tangible-side to the various things that they were trying to transact.

BLOCKCHAIN

Using blockchain protocol and a significant amount of brainpower from a massive team of dedicated developers, they were able to formulate several alternative "tokens" that would resemble these transactions. Through this replication and creation of a new "token," known as 'smart contracts' which will be discussed further in Chapter 8: "Smart Contracts," blockchain was revolutionized to work independently and for many more purposes than simply keeping track of Bitcoin transactions.

ALFORD BENSON

CHAPTER 3
BLOCKCHAIN TECHNOLOGY

Understanding blockchain to the fullest extent means having an understanding of the very technology that makes blockchain a "thing." As you know, blockchain was designed around the same time that Bitcoin was launched. It was later extracted from Bitcoin technology and made capable of standing on its own to serve many other practices. However, what exactly is the blockchain and how does it work? Let us take a closer look at the specific technology behind blockchain.

The Core of Blockchain

At the core of blockchain is a fairly understandable concept. It is, in a sense, a chain of blocks that store information that has been encrypted into the block based on specific information that the block has been given. Specifically, this information revolves around transactions. So, when a transaction of funds, assets, or other information is completed, the transaction is then built into a block and added to the blockchain.

Blockchain is a decentralized network of nodes that are each responsible for protecting the information on the blockchain. This decentralized network means that no node is "in charge." Therefore, if any node is not in agreement with the other nodes, the information being stored in that node is immediately made null and void. It is then automatically and immediately updated with the correct information in the rest of the decentralized network. This keeps them all on the same page and working in a synchronized manner to maintain security and accuracy in the blockchain.

Initially, the blockchain was used to store information about cryptocurrency transactions made with Bitcoin. Now, it is used to store all kinds of information. In the future, it is expected that the types of information that can be stored in this chain will be vast and ever growing. At this point, it primarily revolves around currencies, but it is expected that properties, assets, and other forms of transactional value will eventually make its way into the blockchain. This means that you will be able to transact or trade virtually anything through this network with complete transparency, and free of any risk that may otherwise be associated with these transactions.

What is a "Block?"

As you consider the blockchain, you may be wondering what the "blocks" themselves actually are. The blocks include complex mathematical equations, coding processes, and protocols that are completed to verify the transactional information that is being proposed for the block itself. Once the information is verified, it is stored within the block using an SHA-256 double round hashing process. It is then given a timestamp and added to the blockchain itself. The blockchain is stored in a chronological manner.

Every block that comes after any preexisting block on the blockchain uses information from the previous blocks to generate and validate new blocks. For this reason, you cannot change the information in a previous block without changing all subsequent information. Since this would require a massive amount of time and power on a constantly growing chain, it is virtually impossible. This means that all validated blocks of transactional information are irreversible and are stored on the blockchain forever. There is no way to remove them without disrupting the entire system, which is impossible.

What are Miners?

Miners are those responsible for finding the blocks of transaction in the algorithm, completing the required coding and mathematical processes to validate the block, and then timestamping the blocks and adding them to the blockchain. They are the nodes that make up the decentralized network used to keep the blockchain in operation altogether. Without them, the blockchain would cease to exist.

Since the blockchain is decentralized, it requires many different nodes, or miners, to be involved at all times. Each of these is responsible for not only validating blocks of transactions and storing them in the blockchain, but also for storing the actual blockchain itself. Every single node has the blockchain encrypted within it, in the exact same way as every single node. If anyone were to ever attempt to hack a node and alter the blockchain within it, the blockchain would no longer match the chain stored in other nodes. Therefore, the change would be blocked immediately and the chain would be updated to reflect what was accurate across the entire decentralized system.

ALFORD BENSON

CHAPTER 4
THE PURPOSE OF BLOCKCHAIN

The key purpose of blockchain is to provide an anonymous online ledger that simplifies the way we transact using data. Using blockchain, users can manipulate the ledger in a way that is secure and requires no assistance from a third party.

As it is, most ledgers are connected to a centralized network that is responsible for hosting, manipulating, and maintaining the ledger. For example, the banks that we presently use have centralized systems that manage the money we use, control the completed transactions, and are responsible for protecting user identity. However, based on the nature of the system, they are not entirely secure. User information can still be released, fraud can still happen within the system, and nothing is entirely safe with these systems. Although they are highly secured and monitored, they are not fool-proof and can be hacked by those who have basic knowledge of what they are doing.

Furthermore, despite these systems being centralized, they still require people to actually overlook them and verify transactions. This means that, for various transactions to be approved, someone must be present to actually approve them in the first place. Because of this, transactions can take a significant amount of time and are extremely inconvenient for all involved.

Using blockchain, user information is completely anonymous and, while transactions are made available to the public, no one can see exactly who made the transaction. Instead, they see what the transaction involved and the key-pair of the two users who were responsible for the transaction. If the transaction was denied, it will never be visible on the blockchain, to begin with.

Blockchain reduces the dependency on people and makes transactions far easier and more effective for people who are transacting in the first place. It has the potential to disrupt not only the financial system but also many other systems in place. If blockchain is perfected, it can be used in a massively widespread manner that enables it to facilitate virtually all forms of transactions.

What is the biggest purpose of it?

You now know full well what the various reasons behind blockchain's existence and abilities are, but you may still be wondering what the primary purpose of it is. Luckily, the answer is incredibly simple. The purpose of blockchain is to prevent the usage of centralized systems that can be easily hacked and have its data changed, resulting in fraud for many users of the system. Through blockchain everything is decentralized, and therefore it is virtually impossible to hack the system and adjust the data to change it permanently. Once the remaining nodes in the decentralized system recognize the fraudulent change, the change will be denied and stopped in its tracks. It will never actually be put through or used. It is so secure against hacking that it can be used for higher functions, such as financial and eventually, legal purposes as well.

Is there a secondary purpose?

The second reason why people like blockchain is primarily because of the security. It is rooted in the fact that sometimes, there are transactions that occur between two entities that do not necessarily trust one another. For example, companies in direct competition with one another. Using blockchain, nothing fraudulent can truly take place, resulting in the transaction of data being sound and ensuring that both parties are granted due justice. There are also witnesses to the transactions, preventing anyone from being somehow exposed to fraudulent activity during the transaction.

The biggest purpose of blockchain, no matter what angle you view it from, is security. Through blockchain, everything becomes infinitely more secure. This security is unparalleled anywhere else in ledger-based systems and therefore, it means that blockchain is a massively successful and advanced revolutionary upgrade to a system that deeply needs it. The amount of security it provides to everyone is a form that is highly necessary and not previously experienced anywhere in any system.

CHAPTER 5
HOW BLOCKCHAIN IS CURRENTLY USED

In addition to cryptocurrency itself and providing a safe and secure system for cryptocurrencies to exist within, blockchain provides many other values, too. There are many types of applications in which blockchain can be used in fact.

To date, blockchain is used in several different ways outside of cryptocurrency. Let us explore each of these ways now to get a better sense of how blockchain can be used, how it is currently being used, and in what ways it is already impacting society. This will give you a greater understanding of just how far the blockchain protocol can go, and the many things it can do.

Financial services

As you are already well aware of, the blockchain protocol is phenomenal for the financial industry. While it is currently used as the primary protocol to manage and maintain cryptocurrency, it is also being used to help in existing financial industries as well. Many different credit cards are presently using blockchain as a measure to prevent fraud from taking place.

Although you may not be aware of it, a common phenomenon that takes place with credit cards includes double spending. That is, people use their credit card to purchase a service or product. Then once the merchant delivers, they call their credit card company and have the charge reversed. They do this by saying that they never received their product or service. The merchant then pays the price, losing out on profits.

Through enforcing blockchain, this cannot be done. This prevents people from denying that a transaction took place, from stating that they have been fraudulently charged, or from having transactions reversed when products and services were actually delivered. This is also slowly being integrated into many other financial divisions as well, including standard banks with checking accounts and debit cards.

Smart property

Smart property has smart technology embedded in them, which can make sales and transactions regarding the property easy and irreversible. For example, homes, cars, cookers, company shares, and other tangible and intangible properties can be set up with their own smart technology system. Then they can be connected into the blockchain and transacted as a result. Their smart technology allows them to be seen as a "token" or to have some form of tangible identity that can be traded on the market. Then, once the transaction is complete, it can be embedded in the blockchain and placed on the permanent ledger. This means a more secure way of selling and trading properties.

In addition to being used as a means to sell and trade these items, it can also be used to grant access to the property. For example, someone may have access to a smart key that could grant them access to the property in question, such as granting realtors access to a home. Then once the property is sold, these smart keys would be transferred to the new owner as well. As a result, they would not be fraudulently kept or used by the property's previous owners to grant them unlawful access to the property that is no longer theirs.

This decreases the risk of fraud, mediation fees, and other questionable business transactions that leave a trail of victims in their wake. It also increases the trust between the seller and the buyer and increases efficiency in the transaction process itself.

Smart Contracts

Although we will discuss smart contracts in greater detail in Chapter 8: "Smart Contracts," it is worth introducing right now. After all, smart contracts are presently being used in a variety of areas as a means of taking advantage of blockchain protocol where "If-This-Then-That" (IFTTT) coding is being used.

This contract is unlike a legal contract whereby two parties sign the contract to bind an agreement. Instead, the smart contract is used to facilitate the transaction of something when certain conditions are met. As you will learn, this can include anything from healthcare to government issues.

Identity Protection

Because of the anonymity of blockchain, it provides a wonderful opportunity to secure identity. At this point, blockchain has already been used to design digital passports, certificates (i.e. birth, wedding, and death,) and personal identification such as drivers' licenses. Using blockchain in this way allows people to have private identification that can be tracked and monitored in the blockchain. This allows people to have access to protected identity while still being identifiable for necessary means.

Passports

In 2014 the first ever digital passport was designed and launched, allowing owners to identify themselves both in the online and offline spaces. Essentially, it works by photographing yourself and stamping it with public and private keys. These are both required to prove the passport is legitimate. Then it is stored on a ledger and given an address like Bitcoin's addresses as well as a public IP address. The passport is then confirmed by blockchain users. This allows you to travel with your photograph and key pairs and be easily identified anywhere that you may travel to. It allows every person to be tracked based on where they are going but does not expose the identity of the travelers, outside of the identification process already required for traveling.

Birth, death, and wedding certificates

The documents that prove birth, death, and marriage are highly necessary for anything we do in modern society. There are a variety of rights that we cannot access without these documents. However, they are not presently designed in a way that is extremely secure or safe. They can easily be damaged, replicated, stolen, or destroyed. Using blockchain, however, these certificates can be replaced to make record-keeping far easier for the government.

Personal ID

Using blockchain ID as a digital form of ID would eliminate the need to carry around different identification cards. For example, using it as a driver's license, for your social security, and even for computer passwords or keys. Using this form of ID would make it easier for people to secure their property and items without worrying that they can be stolen or hacked. You would require an individual's private key to gain access, and ideally these keys will only be known by said individual.

Preventing Voter Fraud

The 2016 US presidential election raised many questions in regards to the security of the existing voting system. Using blockchain would make it significantly easier to protect voter's rights and prevent electoral fraud. Every voter would only be able to vote once and would be accounted for through the blockchain. Any illegitimate or fraudulent votes would be instantly denied. Therefore, we could guarantee the safety of voter results in a much more effective way.

ALFORD BENSON

CHAPTER 6
CURRENT LIMITATIONS AND ISSUES

With the technology being quite young, there are still many limitations and issues that are being faced with blockchain. These are things that will be necessary to work out before the protocol can be utilized in a way that would allow it to be fully integrated into modern society. Let us explore what these current limitations and issues are to get a greater idea of what developers are up against, and the issues that must be overcome before blockchain can become integrated further into our modern systems.

Complexity

Integrating blockchain would be rather complex with regards to how the integration itself would work. The technology comes with a vast amount of unknown vocabulary that many people would need to learn to understand what was actually happening. Since the technology would be closely integrated with finances, government, healthcare, and other sensitive sectors, it would be necessary that the entire community learns these new phrases to grasp what was truly taking place.

Furthermore, it would take a lot of effort to overhaul many of the systems that are already in place to replace them with blockchain. Many of the existing systems have been heavily invested in, often seeing thousands, if not millions of dollars of investments taking place. This would require all of these expensive systems to be abandoned for a new, equally expensive system to be integrated. Not only would this be costly, but it would also be heavily rejected by those who are already in these industries. Having to overhaul everything would be a long and expensive process that many would resist for as long as possible. Unless there was an easier and more cost-effective way to integrate blockchain and educate everyone on the new jargon that is used with this technology, fully integrating it is easier said than done.

Network Size

The blockchain is a massive network that grows in size as it responds to attempted attacks on the system. To strengthen a network and keep it safe and secure for everyone to use, a high number of network users are required. If a high number of nodes aren't involved in the system, the system will be lacking in security. This means that many people or nodes would be required to keep the system intact and functional.

Many people are unsure as to whether this will be a flaw that ultimately prevents blockchain from being integrated, or if it is something that can be worked out in some way. The answer one way or another will depend greatly on what developers can learn about blockchain, and how many people are willing to get involved in the network and stay involved to keep it secure.

Network Speed

As vast as the system is for Bitcoin, it is only capable of processing about seven transactions per second. While this may sound rather fast, it is actually incredibly slow when you consider it being integrated on a global scale. For that reason, if blockchain were to become widely integrated, there would have to be a way to turn up the speed and make it even more effective for you to process transactions.

Additionally, if you consider the fact that blockchain is this slow with Bitcoin itself, despite having so many involved in the system, you can imagine how slow it might be if it were integrated into several different systems to be used on a national or international level. An unthinkably high number of nodes would be required to produce mediocre transaction speeds which may never amount to "fast enough" to actually make blockchain worth the switch.

Furthermore, although Bitcoin was praised for being "nearly free" in its earliest days, the transactions have since risen in price. For that reason, it is becoming more costly to complete transactions using Bitcoin. The same would likely happen for blockchain as a whole if it were integrated. This needs to be considered as well.

Human error

Blockchain will permanently store irreversible transactions based on human input. As long as blockchain deems it verified, the transaction is put into the chain and cannot be removed. This is a good thing in many respects, but it does have one major drawback. That is, human error. If a human were to input the parameters of the transaction incorrectly, this could result in an accidental transaction that is not relevant or accurate to what the transaction was intended to be. As a result, this transaction would be permanent and irreversible. While a subsequent transaction could (and hopefully would) be made to compensate for the mistake, it can't possibly be guaranteed. This means that if a transaction was done wrong, someone may potentially lose a significant number of funds or even property as a result of a human error. It would be devastating.

Additionally, if anyone were to accidentally lose their key pairs, they could still be at risk of having someone wipe them out. A private key that accidentally fell into the wrong hands could result in this person taking everything out of the victim's accounts and, since it is irreversible, nothing can be done to restore that person's losses.

51% attack

There is one major security flaw that not many people are aware of when it comes to blockchain. This flaw was initially highlighted by Satoshi Nakamoto when Bitcoin was launched. It is called the "51% attack." This essentially means that if more than 50% of the nodes were in agreement with a lie, the lie would become written as the truth in the blockchain. So, if the blockchain was relied upon for legal and evidential purposes, a lie could technically be integrated as truth and thus true justice can be lost as a result.

Due to the nature of the blockchain, nothing can really be done to avoid this flaw. As long as the majority of systems were in agreement (51% or more,) the information would be passed as truth and the people would be at risk of the lie becoming truth and therefore they could be seriously wronged as a result.

Politics

Since blockchain protocol can digitize the government networks, as well as many other highly sensitive networks, politics definitely comes into play. The idea of having these systems completely decentralized and digitized seems ideal, but it could result in major drawbacks or flaws if it were not integrated properly.

Furthermore, it could result in the government becoming obsolete in some way, taking away their control and potentially resulting in chaos ensuing throughout the country or globe.

There are many disputes between the public and the government in regards to this potential change. Many believe that if you were to digitize the government in this way you may add protection in some respects but you could completely lose it in others. For that reason, it would be necessary for government control to remain somewhat human to prevent potentially fatal errors from taking place and causing major disruption in the country, or worst, on a global scale.

Conclusion

Clearly, there is still much to be worked out in regards to blockchain. Although the technology is wonderful and boasts many positive benefits, there are still many limitations and issues that can result if it were to be integrated into sensitive systems. Some argue that these are nothing compared to the corruption that is already believed to be taking place, but the reality is that the corruption that could come from a young blockchain being prematurely integrated could be far worse.

For blockchain to be fully integrated in the way that people hope it will be, and remain completely secure and honest, it will be necessary that it is integrated slowly. People will need to be patient as developers and researchers explore new ways to secure the system, as well as make it even more efficient and accessible to the variety of industries and sectors that it could be beneficial to.

Ultimately, we must wait for the protocol to mature before we discover whether or not it can actually be integrated into these highly official industries. Despite these limitations and issues, however, there are still many other incredible opportunities for blockchain to be integrated into society to be used in a way that makes it seem highly futuristic. Whether or not it will ever be integrated into these official industries is irrelevant, as the benefits we do stand to gain will still show up in one way or another! You can learn more about how blockchain might change the future of our society in Chapter 10: "Future of Blockchain."

ALFORD BENSON

CHAPTER 7
PERSPECTIVES ON BLOCKCHAIN

When it comes to blockchain, the verdict is still out on what people think about this protocol. While many believe that it can revolutionize the world and change the way society functions, others believe that it will never go further than being a concept. This leaves us with two opposing factions: pro-blockchain, and anti-blockchain. Let us take a look at what people are saying.

Pro-Blockchain

Those who are pro-blockchain are excited about what a future might look like with a decentralized system. They want to know what it would be like to be able to completely manage our own funds free of the banks' influence, and what other types of technology could emerge. These individuals see the many benefits that our society could experience if we were to completely transition everything from healthcare to photo ID over to a blockchain system.

To those who are pro-blockchain, the idea that we could one day park our car on a charging pad and have it pay for its own charge cycle without us having to take out our wallets is fascinating. People have seen how blockchain revolutionized cryptocurrency and made it a fact of our reality, and now they want to see how far they can take it. These are the people who are investing their funds into the research and development of blockchain and who are eagerly awaiting the day when it integrates itself completely. They want to exploit blockchain to its fullest potential and experience all that blockchain has to offer our society.

These individuals realize that blockchain as it is right now, is not strong enough to support all of the things that they desire in a futuristic world, but they do realize that we may be on to the start of something. After all, cryptocurrency was only a concept for over a decade before it officially launched thanks to the blockchain protocol. For that reason, they believe that with enough time and attention, blockchain could become strong enough and powerful enough to actually realize the expectations they have for our futuristic world.

The idea that the current blockchain design could possibly support what they desire to see in the world is not something they fancy. Pro-blockchain defendants do not believe that the present system is enough to support what they are interested in seeing. However, they do believe that we have found the basis for a new protocol or technology that could completely allow us to integrate the digitized systems of the future. For that reason, they are seeking to learn as much as blockchain as they can so that they can learn where and how the system can be strengthened to support future technologies.

It is likely that these individuals will continue to invest in and support the concept of blockchain for many years to come. After all, it was the relentless investment of time, funds, and other resources into cryptocurrency that eventually made it a part of our reality. These individuals believe that the same level of devotion to blockchain could result in it being the very system or the "1.0" version of the very system that will power our entire future.

Anti-Blockchain

The entirely opposite side argues that blockchain will never work and that there is no way that the system would or could ever be integrated on a large scale. These individuals are looking at the history of blockchain and considering why it's not largely popular, and they are looking at the reality of blockchain based on what we know right now. This side of the argument clings more to the reality of what blockchain is right now and are not particularly looking at what the future "could" be with it. Still, they raise many valid points.

First, many anti-blockchain people believe that Bitcoins and cryptocurrency, in general, are just a hype and that soon, no one will be talking about them anymore. For the same reason, they believe they will not be talking about blockchain anymore either. Instead, they believe that they will be on to something new and equally trendy that is just around the corner. "What" it is has yet to be discovered, but ultimately, they do not believe that it will become anything significant.

The next thing they consider is whether or not it is even realistic for large-scale industries like health or government to actually switch over to a completely digitized system. After all, entrusting all of that power to technology may be a bit far-fetched. You never know what could happen, and a massive power outage or some other large-scale system failure could seriously mess everything up. With all of it stored in an online database, one major failure of the system could result in weeks, months, or even years of information being lost. Of course, there are always backup systems, but nothing can guarantee that even those would remain reliable.

Next, there is the worry of the 51% attack. If it was integrated into these highly important systems, one 51% attack filled with false information could be detrimental to the wellbeing of individuals in the healthcare system, or the nation as a whole if the government was involved in these systems.

Finally, another thing is that blockchain can actually be built privately. This means that if the government, healthcare system, or anyone else wanted to privatize their blockchain, this can be done. This would completely eliminate the benefits of "transparency" that many people believe blockchain would be good for.

The reality is that we are simply not yet at a point where we can develop a technology advanced enough to actually replace major industries. It simply cannot happen, as per the argument of anti-blockchainers. While many agree that it is a positive step toward a more united global front, there are still many flaws that need to be worked out. Some believe that this protocol will fail as a whole. Others believe that there is the potential that "something" will come around to fulfill the role that people want blockchain to fulfill, but that it will not be blockchain itself.

Which perspective is right?

Knowing which perspective is right is truly an impossible gamble to make. One thing that both sides seem to agree upon, however, is that blockchain, as it is, will not be able to sustain anything larger than what it is already doing. Unless the technology is improved and advancements are made that allow it to be faster and more secure without the fear of the 51% attack, blockchain simply is not secure or strong enough to wash out entire industries. Not yet, at least.

Whether or not you believe that this technology will one day exist is entirely up to you. What will not change, however, is that people are going to continue to try and bring it to life whether we are on board or not. The best thing to do is to pay attention, continue watching the developments that are made and listen to the rumors and trends that take place in the media. Who knows, one day blockchain may revolutionize the world the same way Bitcoin did to become the official pioneer in the cryptocurrency industry.

ALFORD BENSON

CHAPTER 8
SMART CONTRACTS

You may be wondering why smart contracts have been granted their own chapter. This is because, like decentralized apps, smart contracts are a major revolution in the blockchain developments and have a massive impact on how blockchain works. As you already know, smart contracts are not like traditional contracts where two parties sign a binding agreement. Instead, they are contracts that are set in place that is built in the "If-This-Then-That" (IFTTT) protocol. This means that when predetermined conditions are met, something specific will happen. For example, when a certain date and time is reached, a set number of funds will be released to a previously chosen party. The realm of possibilities with smart contracts is massive, and what can be done with them is incredible.

What is a smart contract?

A smart contract is basically a digitized agreement or parameter that assists in facilitating the transaction of some form of property between two individuals. The form of property that can be traded varies, from homes to money, to shares in a company, or virtually anything else with transactional value. The way this transaction works through a smart contract is by providing a conflict-free way of transacting goods between two people without requiring a middleman.

Essentially, smart contracts render lawyers, bankers, and other advisors unnecessary in the transaction of major properties or goods. Think of a smart contract like a vending machine. Basically, with a vending machine, you would drop a coin in the machine and be given whatever you have "ordered" from it. There is no need for a salesperson or a cashier. When it comes to smart contracts, you drop a Bitcoin into the "vending machine" and are in exchange given property, escrow, a driver's license, or anything else into your account. There is no need for a notary, lawyer, or anyone else to sign and validate your document and guarantee its legitimacy. This is all done through the blockchain and smart contracts.

Smart contracts are not merely a transaction, however. There is a lot of protection that comes with them. Each smart contract is created with its own rules and penalties that are structured around the agreement. This is where the term "contract" comes into play. Thanks to these rules and penalties, there are clearly defined structures that lay the parameters for how the system will work and how the transaction will take place. If the parameters are not met or someone goes against them, the transaction will cease to exist. Unlike written agreements, however, a smart contract will automatically uphold and enforce the obligations laid out in the contract. There is no way to get around it or commit fraud against the other party once you have agreed to the contract and validated your "part" in it.

For a smart contract to work, two parties would agree upon a set of parameters for the agreement. The agreement and assets involved in the agreement are then transferred into a program where the program will run a series of code over the agreement. Once it has validated the agreement, the conditions will automatically be validated and then the assets will be delivered accordingly. This is all based on the coding that is set within the parameters of the smart contract. As previously stated, once you enter the contract, you cannot pull out or otherwise stop the agreement from taking place. The only way that it can be voided is if the agreements or conditions were not met and so the contract itself was deemed null and void. If the contract was deemed null and void, the assets would immediately be transferred back to their original owners and no official "swap" of assets would be put through. In other words, nothing would change and it would be as though the contract never existed, to begin with.

Let us take a look at an example of what a smart contract might look like, imagine that you are planning to rent a home and you choose to do so through the usage of smart contracts, blockchain, and Bitcoin. Basically, the parameters would be set that once you transferred the first month's rent to the landlord by the specified date, you would automatically be given the digital key to gain access to the apartment and the funds would automatically be deposited into the landlord's account. Alternatively, if you failed to provide the funds by the specified date, the key would remain in the landlord's name and you would automatically be refunded your fees if any were paid. So, if the correct parameters were not met, nothing would be issued and there would be no fraud or negative impact on anyone. Aside of course, from you not gaining access to the space you intended to rent!

How smart contracts can be used

There are many ways that smart contracts can be used in the future if they were given proper attention. These ways include involvement with the government, management, in supply chains, real estate, healthcare, and even with automobiles!

Government

With the government, using smart contracts will help further secure the voting system to ensure that it was justified and accurate for what voters truly wanted. While many claim that the present voting system is highly safe, it is difficult for many who are in the public to agree with or accept that. For some, they struggle to believe the government and thus in many cases, recounts are demanded. Unfortunately, there is no way for the public to feel entirely sure that they are being properly represented by their government.

If smart contracts were used the ledger-protected votes will be impossible to tamper, therefore there would be no possible way for anyone to deny the outcome - government or public alike. Additionally, smart contracts could result in the turnout for voting day being significantly higher. As it is, voters are required to wait in heinous lineups for several hours to cast their vote. Many are not interested in waiting, and so they end up not actually attending the voting polls. Through using smart contracts, it would become a lot easier for people to vote because it would be done quickly, efficiently, and without massive lineups.

Management

Using smart contracts with business and management would be a great way to effectively distribute the workload and avoid arguments or quarrels over which work is to be done by whom.

Once the contracts are enforced, people would simply have to do the work assigned to them. This would be an accurate, transparent, and automated system that would make managing a team of employees significantly easier.

As it is, there is a lot of back-and-forths required for individuals to complete their work. Managers are often providing their employees with more and more information to ensure that they know what is expected of them. With smart contracts, however, all of this information would be placed into the contract and given to the team. It would streamline the workflow and make it significantly easier to eliminate discrepancies that often take place with independent processing. Furthermore, if used properly, it can eliminate potentially costly lawsuits that occasionally arise as a result of improperly completed workflow tasks.

Supply Chains

Supply chains are often overwhelmed by the paper system, completely unsure as to what they need to produce more of, and what is not selling well. As a result, they often tend to produce too much of products that are not particularly popular, and not enough of those that are selling out rapidly. Through smart contracts, if a delivery system brought a product, the contract would then signify that the product was delivered. Then, this would trigger information to be passed up the chain and delivered to the supply chain themselves. As a result, they would know to produce more of the products that were selling out quickly, and less of those that were not as popular. This would not only help with ensuring that products are available in a timely and convenient manner but will also prevent waste as a result of having too many products that aren't selling as well.

Real Estate

Using smart contracts mean that you can easily transact real estate using them. You can either rent your apartments or facilities directly or even sell them directly. As it is, we need to pay advertisers to advertise rental space, and realtors to sell properties. Using smart contracts, however, there would be no reason to hire either. Instead, you create a smart contract on the ledger that would state that once fees are paid, the next action which is either the delivery of the key or escrow, would be delivered to the recipient. The transaction would be completely secured and will not be completed unless both parties had contributed their unique elements of the process.

Once your key and information are in the public ledger, people would be able to see you there if you wanted them to. The system is anonymous, but you can choose to become known if you prefer. For that reason, you can attach your realtor information to the transaction and every time one was completed it would become available for public viewing. People could simply go into the system, seek out realtors or rental agencies, and communicate with you directly. It would simplify the transactional process and serve as an additional free mode of marketing to get the word out there about your company.

Health Care

If the blockchain and smart contracts were used in health care, you would be able to access your personal health records effortlessly. Rather than carry around a health card and have doctors retrieve information from previous doctors, everything would be available immediately. So, say you were hospitalized due to an accident, your medical team will immediately be aware of all of your previous health information based on what was made available through your private key and smart contract. As a result, they would be able to treat you more effectively and accurately, without making any mistakes that can be easily avoided.

As it is, many times doctors are left guessing. They have to wait for information to be administered from office to office. If you were in an emergency, they may not have time to wait for your medical records to be sent over from your doctor's office. This presently results in some individuals being given the wrong information or medication, which could easily be prevented if all of your information was made available immediately.

Automobiles

Automobiles are another wonderful way for smart contracts to come to life. Through the use of smart contracts, automobiles can easily be sold from one person to another once the proper funds are provided. This is not the only way, however.

BLOCKCHAIN

Through smart contracts, the vehicle you own and drive could become completely automated. Using the IFTTT technology, they could create self-driving, self-parking cars. The vehicle would be able to know who was "at fault" in an accident and determine a variety of information based on your vehicle. They could also assist you in being charged lower insurance rates based on how you drive, which would all be documented by your vehicle's smart contracts. Furthermore, you could simply park your vehicle on a charging pad and, if you had permitted it, your vehicle would pay for itself to be charged up for your next cycle. This would make it significantly easier for you to complete anything you desire with your vehicle, making owning and driving a car even easier than it already is.

ALFORD BENSON

CHAPTER 9
DECENTRALIZED APPS

A decentralized app, often known as a DApp, is an application that runs through a peer-to-peer network of computers as opposed to running solely through a single computer. These DApps have existed since peer-to-peer networks were introduced and are designed to exist on the internet in a way where no particular entity controls or owns them.

What is a Decentralized App?

Presently, thousands of software systems already exist as a means for performing a variety of different functions. For example, Bitcoin miners use software that allows them to verify and validate Bitcoin transactions. There are many different reasons why software exists and in online space, they fulfill many different purposes.

Traditional software is designed to exist on a centralized system. This is a server-client model where the individual installs the software directly onto their computer and it runs privately in their own system. Although the software may be downloaded by millions of people, their unique download of the software will only work for them, privately.

Decentralized software, however, is different. This software runs from a series of different nodes and is transmuted out to various other nodes, or systems. Decentralized applications that are closed-source are typically run by many different servers but can't be manipulated or changed by "just anyone." Instead, you must have prior and specific permissions to manipulate or change the application. In this case, the users who download the software must trust that the developer is being honest when they say it is decentralized.

Alternatively, open-source DApps are ones that can be downloaded and changed by anyone. This means that anyone who downloads the application or software can make changes to the software itself. Through blockchain, the updates and changes are all stored in the chain so that everyone can see when and where these changes were made, and who made them.

DApps are created by a central developer at first but are then decentralized across many systems to make them available for several other developers to adjust or change. This is how they become decentralized in the first place.

The alternative to decentralized software is distributed software. Many people are unaware of what the difference is between decentralized apps and distributed apps. Decentralized, as you know, means that many different people have access to the ability to change and modify the app itself. The app is then downloaded by others who are not actually involved in modifying the application. For decentralized apps, no single node is "in charge." Instead, a series of nodes are "in charge" and are responsible for the application's management. For distributed applications, this simply means that they are spread across many nodes instead of just one.

Based on the structure of these two formats, an application can be both decentralized and distributed at the same time.

Bitcoin, for example, is an application that is distributed based on the fact that it exists on a timestamped public ledger. However, it is also decentralized because if a single node fails, the rest will continue to uphold and maintain the system. If Bitcoin were only distributed but not decentralized, if one node failed, they would all fail and the entire system would be down until the node was repaired.

Future of Decentralized Apps

Decentralized applications provide many benefits to users. Primarily, they are incapable of being attacked or hacked. This means that any software or application built in a decentralized manner is infinitely easier and safer for you to access, versus any other application that has a centralized system. It requires an enormous amount of power to attack a decentralized system. For the most part, this power is not actually feasible nor accessible to anyone, so there is really no way to hack into the decentralized system. If you do hack into one of the decentralized nodes, the rest will recognize the discrepancy created in the node and will simply reject the attempted change to the system.

Decentralized applications prevent users from being exploited in any particular way. Because there is no one in charge and no one responsible for holding the "majority" of the share in the application, a singular entity can't exploit the system for their own personal gain. This means they can't take or sell your information or adjust the program or software to suit their own personal benefits at the expense of anyone else's.

There are presently many applications being used in a DApp manner, each of which gives us an example of how DApps can assist us in building a safer future online. Some of these DApps include companies that provide micro-loans, social media companies, cloud storage, crowdfunding services, and more. Essentially, by having all of these on decentralized platforms, people cannot be exploited for personal gain. None of your information can be stolen or distributed, you are not going to end up paying fees to the application to perform various functions, and your private identity and information are kept private and safe. They cannot be sold for personal gain by the developer. As it is, virtually every centralized system in effect at this time exploits your information in one way or another for personal gain. Many social media websites and search engines, for example, track your keywords and searches to target advertisements toward you based on your personal browsing history. While this does not mean much to a lot of people, it can be considered a breach of privacy to some. However, when we sign up for or use these services, we are in turn providing consent for this action to take place. This means that we cannot actually treat it as a breach of privacy because we have already given consent.

CHAPTER 10
FUTURE OF BLOCKCHAIN

Blockchain has a fairly unknown future, but many have speculated on what it may look like. It is important to note that blockchain itself is merely software, so considering the future with blockchain requires us to consider ways that blockchain may be integrated into various technologies to shape the way we live our lives. Note that when we explore what has already been fantasized about the future with blockchain, we are actually considering what the integration of this technology into other technologies could mean for how we live our lives in the future.

Asset Management

Current asset management systems can be risky for those who are seeking to trade or sell assets.

This process can be expensive and can expose the traders to great risk, making it difficult to determine whether or not the process will be legitimate or viable until it is already completed. This can expose those involved in the trade to fraudulent activities that could cost them major in the long run. This risk is amplified when we consider cross-border trades or transactions.

For the current system, there are various parties involved in the trade who each keep their own records of the trade. This means that there is a significant risk of error, where people may possess different records. At that point, it would be difficult to determine who was correct and who was false in the discrepancy.

Using the blockchain ledger allows these records to be encrypted, making them absolute and automatically the same across the entire board. This means that the process would be simplified and that intermediaries (broker, custodian, settlement manager, etc.) would not be required in the transaction. So, this also saves those involved in the transaction a significant fee that would have otherwise been paid to the asset management team responsible for ensuring the transaction was not exposed to possible fraud.

In addition to the blockchain ledger, smart contracts could simplify the process even more. Both parties could "deposit" their assets into the system and, following the completion of the coding check, the system would validate the transaction and submit the appropriate assets to either end of the transaction. This would ensure the trade was fair and that the proper parameters were met. It would avoid fraudulent transactions. If one party failed to uphold their promised or required end of the transaction, it simply would not happen. This means that one person would not send their asset while the other person fails to uphold their end of the transaction. For example, sending a significant amount of cash to one party only for them to keep the cash but not send the promised products or fulfill the service that was agreed upon.

Using blockchain and smart contracts could significantly reduce the impact and risk imposed on those involved in the transaction no matter where the receiving parties are located. This would make national, international, and global trades of any magnitude infinitely safer, less time consuming and far more cost effective for those involved.

Insurance Claims

Claims processing can be extremely difficult. It is a process that can be frustrating for both parties involved in the claim, as well as the processor themselves. Using the traditional form, the processor is required to wade through many different claims that have been made to ensure that the company is not being exposed to fraud. They must also sort through fragmented data sources, as well as abandoned policies and many frustrating situations. This can make processing claims in the insurance division extremely difficult and infuriating for the claims processor themselves. It also slows down the completion of the claim which can be frustrating and difficult for those who are actually making the claim. Some people who made a claim on their vehicle insurances, for example, had waited over five years for the claim to be settled.

Using the blockchain system, the claims could be processed quickly and in a transparent, hassle-free and risk-free environment. These claims would be made, and then the blockchain could allow insurers to quickly capture the ownership of assets that are being insured and could also quickly tap into all of the information of the insured assets and individuals. This would make accessing the information required to process claims significantly faster, and easier. They would have a trail of information associated with both the insured asset and the individual who insured the asset. Then they could quickly process the claim in accordance with the gathered information. There would be no need to go back-and-forth and dig through tons of documents and files to acquire all of the necessary information to process the claims.

Cross-Border Payments

Paying across borders with the traditional system can be slow, expensive, and prone to errors. Furthermore, they are susceptible to money laundering, where people use overseas accounts to hide their dirty money and then send it back to themselves to be used at a later date, with the paper trail of the money erased. Or created, if the money was acquired "under the table."

In addition to the many risks this money is exposed to, it also takes an incredibly lengthy amount of time to process the payment. Using the blockchain, these transactions could be completed quickly and without the requirement of several different individuals being present to validate and approve of the transaction. Furthermore, if there was a reason to believe that the transaction was fraudulent, the system would immediately shut it down and prevent it from taking place, to begin with. So, the risk of fraud would be significantly reduced, the time frame would be shortened, and to top it off, the fees associated with the process would be minimized as well.

Revolutionized Lending System

Presently, lending money or receiving loans can be somewhat difficult. There is a lengthy and thorough process that must be undertaken to acquire a loan. As a private lender, you may be worried that you are not protected by the same means that public lenders, such as banks, are protected by. For that reason, you may be reluctant to provide any form of assistance to those who may be interested in lending money. Even if you have the funds to lend, the idea itself may seem too risky to actually take part in. Many companies exist that allow you to lend money, but often they take a large chunk of the interest you earn, meaning that you earn significantly less through these resources.

Using smart contracts and blockchain, unconventional lending could become a reality in the future. Anyone with money could lend to anyone who needs money, and they would use smart contracts to facilitate the lending process. As a result, these lenders could earn back money through interest if they wanted to. Alternatively, they could lend the money and choose to charge no interest rate at all. It would be entirely up to them.

This would mean that lenders have access to this option, while those in need of a loan would have greater access to loans as well. As it is, if a person hits bankruptcy or loses their home because they cannot afford the loan plus the enormous interest rates, there is not a lot that they can do. Their credit is damaged as a result and it can take a long time to rebuild the credit and protect themselves from future disaster. It can truly create a state of financial ruin for a person and take away their entire livelihood along with the safety and comfort of their home. In many cases they also lose their means of transportation, making their attempts at attaining a decent livelihood even more difficult. These situations happen all of the time, and they can be extremely devastating to affected individuals and families.

Through smart contracts and blockchain, these individuals will have easy access to money. The property, which would be listed as smart property, could be held as collateral by the lender. Then as long as the loan continues to be paid back, there would be no reason for the collateral to be kept by the lender. However, if the loan was not paid back, the lender will be able to take possession of the house. There would be no need for the lender to be shown any information regarding credit or work history because the entire parameter of the loan was outlined in the smart contract. The many documents required to be processed at this point are rendered unnecessary, and the entire process would be significantly easier and less time-consuming. Furthermore, this would be encoded on the blockchain ledger for all to see, meaning there would be no way for the lender or borrower to create a false claim or otherwise attempt to defraud the other party.

Revolutionizing Primitive Smart Property

At this time, smart property already exists. For example, the key fob you use to get into your car. If it has an immobilizer, for example, the immobilizer can only be activated once you tap a certain key on the fob. Alternatively, your smartphone likely has a PIN associated with it. It can only be accessed or activated once the PIN has been entered into the device to unlock it. Both of these use cryptography to protect your ownership over the property, and both represent a primitive form of smart property.

Primitive smart property is an incredible revolution on its own, but it does come with some drawbacks. For example, if you lose the fob or your phone, you cannot easily transfer or copy the information from it. This means that if it's lost, it will have to be replaced completely. This can be expensive, and also frustrating if you had anything important or sentimental on your device.

If these devices were integrated with modern smart property protocol, the information would be digitized and would be attached to your "account." This means that you could input a certain key pair into your "account" and all of the information that was lost on the device would instantaneously be available to you. You could also render the device itself null and void, so no one would be able to use it to access any information or use it for malicious purposes. Any lost protocol could be replicated and replaced, and your lost information would immediately be restored, no hassle and no risk involved.

Internet of Things (IoT) Blockchain

We can all agree that any material object can also be classified as a "thing." When it has an on and off switch that allows it to be connected to the internet and to other "things," it becomes an "Internet of Things." When the thing itself is connected to the internet, whether it is a car, computer, refrigerator, or otherwise, it becomes more than merely an object. At this point, it is now involved in the people-to-people, people-to-things, and things-to-things network. This may sound confusing but hang on. It will make sense in a moment, I promise!

Once it is connected to the Internet of Things, your objects can begin to automatically do things on their own. For example, a printer can order cartridges when it runs low, an alarm clock can trigger your coffee pot to start brewing based on whatever time you set the alarm clock for, your fridge can order more food if it is low, and so forth. These transactions are facilitated through the Internet of Things, can be activated using the IFTTT technology of smart contracts, and are then stored in the blockchain once the transaction is completed. That way, all of it is stored in a public ledger that proves the transactions were completed and legit. It is also subject to your approval, meaning you can change the IFTTT settings to change the way the protocol works. So, if you want to stop your printer from ordering its own cartridges, for example, you would simply change or deactivate the smart contract.

This has the capacity to work on a small, independent scale as stated above. However, it also has the capacity to work by integrating entire "smart cities." These would assist cities in having a cleaner and safer environment that is also more energy efficient. Since the IFTTT smart contracts could be set to trigger certain events, they could preserve energy, funds, and other resources right down to specific quantities. This would mean our cities would become healthier, safer, and more environmentally friendly. It would also all be stored in the blockchain, making it visible to all on the public ledger.

The Outlook

The idea of a future with blockchain is incredible. There are many fascinating upgrades that could take place as a result of the integration of blockchain technology. However, at this time, it is not likely that these changes will occur in the very near future. As previously discussed, it will take time for the protocol to be developed enough that it can be a viable option to be used on a wider scale. Hopefully, as we continue to explore the technology and the many uses it has, we can continue to search for a way that blockchain can become more prevalent and used in a greater way. The idea of having a complete smart home with a smart city and many other advantages is one that seems highly ideal and beneficial to all.

ALFORD BENSON

CHAPTER 11
BLOCKCHAIN TERMINOLOGY

Blockchain is a technology with many different terms which are not commonly understood by those who are not too savvy on what exactly the technology is. To help you understand the terms used within this book, as well as terms that you may have come across elsewhere when researching blockchain, I have included a section dedicated to teaching you about blockchain terminology. This will boost your confidence in understanding information you read about blockchain itself. It will also help you further understand the terminology used in blockchain-related programs, such as cryptocurrencies and DApps.

The blockchain Altcoin

An abbreviated version of the term "alternative coin," suggesting that the coin is an alternative to Bitcoin. These coins typically operate on the blockchain system but are not a part of Bitcoin itself.

Bitcoin

Bitcoin is a cryptocurrency that runs on a peer-to-peer global network that is decentralized, open sourced, and bypasses middlemen by enabling anyone to A piece of data stored within a "block" of coding that is linked with other blocks to form the entire blockchain. The data stored within the block memorizes what took place prior to that block being created, meaning that each block is chronological and created based off of data and information stored in the previous block. They have complex mathematical equations that must be solved to validate the blocks, which enables them to be added to the chain.and can be used by anyone who has access to a smartphone or computer.

Blockchain

This is a shared public ledger that records transactions in a chronological order. Anyone can inspect it or view information on the ledger, but no one is in control over it. It is protected against hacking and related security risks and is built in a secure format.

Block

A piece of data stored within a "block" of coding that is linked with other blocks to form the entire blockchain. The data stored within the block memorizes what took place prior to that block being created, meaning that each block is chronological and created based off of data and information stored in the previous block. They have complex mathematical equations that must be solved to validate the blocks, which enables them to be added to the chain.

Block Explorer

A tool that is available online to explore the blockchain for particular transactions. You can also watch live transactions as they are added and analyze the chain for any desired information.

Block Reward

A predetermined value of cryptocurrency rewarded to miners for processing transactions in given blocks. By rewarding individuals who are involved in mining, it encourages them to mine and stay on a part of the network responsible for making blockchain a decentralized and legitimate system.

Chain Linking

The process of connecting two blocks on the blockchain. This allows blockchain blocks to communicate with sidechains and other blocks within the chain to exchange assets and information between the blocks freely.

Cloud Mining

Modern mining practices that do not require the extreme level of hardware and

money into the company that already has a system of mining networks in place and receive a share of the revenue earned from the company. This form of mining has a low return compared to classical mining but requires lower startup investment and lower monthly fees due to not using your own electricity and equipment.

Consensus

The agreement between all of the nodes involved in maintaining the blockchain. All blockchain nodes must reach a consensus that either approves or denies a block of transaction. These protocols allow nodes to communicate with one another and agree on a single value, or consensus, enabling the block to be considered accurate and legitimate.

Consortium Blockchain

The consensus process in a consortium blockchain is controlled by pre-selected nodes. For example, if a financial institution was using the blockchain for their own purposes, they would have pre-selected nodes within their institution responsible for managing their own sidechain. This will allow them to void the requirement of all nodes, and only require the consensus of their own nodes within their own network.

Cryptojacking

The secret use of a device for mining cryptocurrency. This essentially means that a device gets into the cryptocurrency network but masks itself. So, any time a person logs onto their website through their browser, the website begins using their browser and machine to mine cryptocurrencies. They are essentially taking over the browser and using it for their own mining purposes. The best way to make sure this is not happening to you is to look into unusual CPU behavior or debug your console. If done properly, the cryptojacking can take place even if you are no longer on their website as the bug entered your browser itself.

DApp

Decentralized applications, or applications and software that are managed by a decentralized system. This system is run just like the blockchain system itself, through a series of nodes that are each responsible for working together to store information regarding the application or software.

Fiat Currency

Money that is declared by the government for meeting financial obligations. These are often considered "traditional currencies," and include ones like the USD, EUR, GBP, and CAD. They are ones that are recognized by the government as "true" currencies.

Genesis Block

The first block to ever exist in the blockchain.

Light Node

A computer on the decentralized blockchain network that is only responsible for verifying a limited number of transactions. Typically, these will be relevant to the dealings of the node and will use the simplified payment verification (SPV) mode to complete a transactional verification process.

Mining

The process of adding blocks of transaction to the public ledger. These are specifically used in Bitcoin. The ledger itself is known as blockchain. The miners are responsible for verifying blocks of transaction and completing complex mathematical equations and coding processes to ensure the blocks are properly verified, timestamped, and added to the blockchain.

Mining Pool

A group of miners who come together and combine their computing powers to increase their mining output and maximize profits. They share profits between them, increasing their earning potential and overall revenue.

Node

Any computer that is connected to the blockchain is referred to as a node. These are all important in the process of enforcing the rules of blockchain. Full nodes are the backbone of the network and are responsible for enforcing all the rules and distributing information in the system. Lightweight nodes on the other hand, only perform certain functions.

Oracles

These are responsible for existing between the smart contracts on the blockchain and the "outside world." They provide the data required to prove the performance of the smart contract while ensuring that the commands are sent to external systems. They play an important role in the functionality of smart contracts.

Private Blockchains

The ledger of a private blockchain is only shown to a single organization. Read permissions may be completely public or may have certain restrictions. The types of restrictions that can be held are not complete, so parts will still be public. These are commonly used in single companies or organizations for their private databases.

Private and Public Key Pairs

A public-private key pair is generated every single time a user sets up a cryptocurrency wallet. The private key is a randomly generated number that enables this user to use the blockchain for transactional purposes. They use this key to access their own wallet, and this key is kept protected and private to the individual. The public key is the one that is made available to others for transactional purposes. The private key should never be shared.

Public Blockchains

These are ledgers of blockchain that are completely public and that typically exist on a public scale. For example, the blockchain associated with Bitcoin would be a public blockchain. Anything commonly used and accessed by the public would be considered a public blockchain.

Satoshi Nakamoto

The person or group responsible for creating Bitcoin protocol. The currency was described and released in a published paper in 2008, then launched publicly in 2009. This person or group of people remain anonymous behind the alias Satoshi Nakamoto.

Smart Contracts

Computer protocols that are used to facilitate pre-negotiated transaction details automatically. They enforce the parameters that have been predetermined by two parties and ensure that assets are traded properly.

Sidechains

These are blockchains that operate among one another as well as with the Bitcoin blockchain. They operate alongside Bitcoin and can interact with the Bitcoin blockchain but do not directly impact the Bitcoin blockchain information.

Token

These are a form of digital identification provided for various properties or assets that enable them to be traded on the blockchain. Blockchain requires some form of digital identity for anything to be traded. Without a token attached to smart property, smart contracts, cryptocurrency, or any other asset, a transaction would not be processed and shown in the blockchain.

Testnet

This is a form of test blockchain where new versions of client software are tested on the blockchain without actually putting any form of real value at risk on it. Since the transactions are not reversible, developers would not want to test in real time with real value, as this would not make sense.

Wallet

This is the digital file where a person's keys and digital communications are stored with their corresponding blockchain. These contain keys, not coins, and are important for storing the information regarding how much coins each person has. These wallets come in two forms: hot wallets that are connected to the internet and cold wallets which aren't. The cold wallets are considered "back-up" versions of the wallets and protect an individual's assets from potential theft.

51% Attack

This is a condition where upward of half of the existing nodes are in agreement with false information. This could take place if a malicious group of miners owned half of the computing power of the blockchain and chose to input malicious information into it for the purpose of creating truth from false transactions. As long as the group controls 51% or more of the computing power they can input false transactions and disrupt the entire network. This would be considered an attack, much like a hack. This person could spend the same coin many times, stop other people's transactions from being approved, or otherwise maliciously intervene with the network.

ALFORD BENSON

CONCLUSION

Over the past decade, many new technologies have been released for public use. Among those technologies was Bitcoin, which simultaneously resulted in the introduction of blockchain protocol. Blockchain is the protocol that actually made Bitcoin possible. It was the protocol that made this the first ever cryptocurrency that was sound, secure, and could be used on a wide scale.

Indeed, Blockchain taught us several ways to earn money. We can earn big time by mining for cryptocurrencies, by building our firms on a blockchain, by becoming a blockchain expert, and by investing and trading in cryptocurrency. There are several ways to earn money!

Because of how successful blockchain has been with Bitcoin, many developers were eager to research this protocol further to see what other ways it could be used in technology. Researchers and developers wanted to know how they could exploit this technology and take advantage of it to the fullest, getting as much as possible out of it.

I hope that this book was able to provide you with plenty of information regarding blockchain, including what the protocol actually is, and why it's so revolutionary. While the true future of blockchain remains unknown and many are still debating whether or not it is here to stay, it is safe to say that it has introduced us to something we have never experienced or witnessed before. Through the introduction of blockchain, we have become closer than ever before to integrate a system of new protocol and software that can allow us to lead the type of future that once only existed in the realms of science-fiction.

From enabling us to block out the need for middlemen in all forms of transactions from legal documents to financial transactions to help us put smart contracts and IFTTT technology to use for amazing purposes, blockchain has introduced us to a lot. Whether or not blockchain itself will revolutionize our future and bring these realities into existence is almost no longer necessary.

BLOCKCHAIN

What is important is that we realize that we are merely a few years away from being able to fully integrate these technologies in a sound and reliable manner. The more researchers and developers continue to invest in the technology, the more we will come to understand it. As a result, either blockchain will be upgraded to take on these new integrations or an entirely new system that is built based on what we have learned from it. Either way, this future can no longer be denied.

Blockchain has changed the way geeks do computer programming. Several firms and businesses today still rely on the client-server model used when the Internet boom despite the risks that it has like server failures, traffic overload, and hacks. These problems were fixed by the blockchain technology – thanks to Satoshi Nakamoto who first introduced Bitcoin in a white paper where blockchain was first heard of.

As you have learned, blockchain may sound complicated, but as you continue to study it, analyze the basics, and understand how it works, you will get to know it more easily. Blockchain has changed our world – our technology –

significantly. It improved how transactions are being held, how businesses run, and how to keep our funds safe. It is indeed a very interesting technology we should study and embrace.

The next thing to do is to continue paying attention to blockchain and how it continues to be integrated into our society. As more research and development is carried out, we are seeing this protocol integrated into more and more ways. Already, about 15% of the banks in America are using blockchain protocol to support their systems. It is only a matter of time before it takes over completely!

Lastly, if you enjoyed "Blockchain: A Clear and Simple Guide to the Technology That Makes Cryptocurrencies Work," and felt like it taught you a lot about blockchain, I ask that you please review it on Amazon Kindle. Your honest feedback would be greatly appreciated.

www.ingramcontent.com/pod-product-compliance
Lightning Source LLC
Chambersburg PA
CBHW070153230526
45471CB00002B/637